Tony, Tony, Tony!

Tony, Tony, Tony!

"Tails" of an Italian greyhound

Donna Clementoni

Writers Club Press
San Jose New York Lincoln Shanghai

Tony, Tony, Tony!
"Tails" of an Italian greyhound

Writers Club Press
an imprint of iUniverse, Inc.

For information address:
iUniverse, Inc.
5220 S. 16th St., Suite 200
Lincoln, NE 68512
www.iuniverse.com

Illustrated by Mario Clementoni

ISBN: 0-595-21879-2

Printed in the United States of America

Dedicated to Tony,
a 91/2 pound
continuous bundle of joy

"I marvel that such small ribs as these hold such a vast desire to please."

Ogden Nash

Shhhh!!!!

He has no idea that
he's a dog!…

Welcome to Tony's World!

Hi! My name is Tony. I am an Italian Greyhound who was born in Lawton, Oklahoma with my 3 brothers.

Life was frightening at first…everything was new and unfamiliar…but I stayed safe and secure, cuddled up with my mother and brothers while my father looked on. Most of the time we'd sleep…then eat…then play a little…and sleep, again!

At night, when we were snuggled up, together, my parents would tell us stories about our ancient ancestors.

They lived with famous people...pharaohs and kings and queens...in exotic places like Egypt and Italy.

We are the oldest breed of hunting dogs. Rats were our favorite thing to chase!

We didn't begin in Italy but the Italians "drew" attention to us by painting us on canvases and sculpting statues that looked like us.

My Aunt Vickie & Uncle Bob thought that was such a good idea that they had an artist paint a portrait of ME!

Way back when, houses didn't have heat like they do now.

Italian Greyhounds, like myself, kept their "family" warm by curling up beside them in bed.

Our body temperature is much warmer then human's. It averages 101 degrees. We're doggie heating pads!

I'm so proud I come from royalty!!!

At night I dream that I am the pampered pet of a famous king or queen.

All the other dogs in the kingdom, no matter how big and mean, are VERY nice to me!

Many centuries later, my "bigger relatives", the Greyhounds, became famous for racing…chasing a little mechanical rabbit around a track! They are very fast! I look a lot like them except MUCH SMALLER.

When they "retired" from racing, loving families would adopt them so that they could rest and relax for the rest of their lives.

People tease them and say that they are "couch potatoes" because they can sleep all day!

A lot of dogs of different breeds like to "show-off" how handsome or pretty or obedient they are.

They compete in shows for ribbons.

My daddy was a champion! He won a ribbon for 'best in breed" at a show in his town. His formal name is *Marchwind Dark Gift* but his friends call him *Sable* because that's what color he is.

I am not going to compete in shows (I can't sit still that long) and I am also not going to have children when I grow up.

There are enough puppies without homes...I don't need to bring more into the world!

Now back to my beginnings…

When I was 12 weeks and could eat regular puppy food and didn't need to be with my mommy all the time, my human friend, Kelly, decided it was time to find me a home and family all of my own.

She put an announcement on the Internet to let people know my brothers and I were looking to be adopted.

Many, many miles away, in Ellicott City, Maryland, a woman was looking for an Italian greyhound puppy.

She called Kelly and spent a lot of time learning about *"Iggy's"* (that's a nickname for Italian greyhounds). After deciding we were the right dog for her family she asked to see a picture.

Through the magic of computers, Kelly "e-mailed" a picture of one of one of my brothers and me.

I WON! Something about my cute face made my new mommy, Donna, pick me!!!

Don't be sad for my brother...he was quickly adopted to a nice home in Illinois.

Kelly took me to the airport, introduced me to the pilot (I wanted to ride with him ☹) and put me in a puppy carrier for the plane ride to Maryland.

I was sooo scared! My whole body shook and I wrapped myself up in a little ball to keep warm and stay safe.

The world suddenly seemed really big and scary!

It was the first time I was away from my mother and father and brothers☹!

After all, I only weighed 4.4lbs and I was still a BABY!

When the big plane landed a man put the crate (with me in it peeking out the door) on the baggage conveyor.

My eyes lit up and my ears stood up when I saw this lady waving at me with a big, big smile on her face. My new mommy!

She took me out of the crate, wrapped me in a warm blanket and hugged and kissed me.

Ever so slowly, I stopped shaking.

I had a feeling everything would be OKAY!

It's funny…when I get scared my tail automatically curls under my legs.

I can't help it!

Everyone knows right away when I'm nervous.

I'm soooo OBVIOUS!

Mommy and I and my new granddad, who they call *"Motts"*, drove me to my new home.

I thought "I am special!" I was going to live in a BIG house like the relatives I heard about.

The house was on a hill and there were even goldfish swimming in a pond half way up the lawn.

I would visit them later! First I went to explore the inside of my new home.

After all, was December and I don't like the cold!

I think I'm going to LOVE it here!

I have soft, cuddly ball beds on all three floors of the house. I take lots of naps and when I'm done…watch out! I run fast and I love to play!

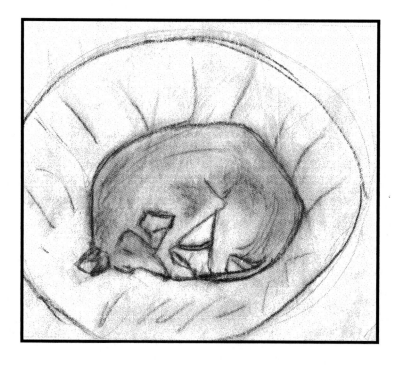

There are lots of steps in my new home.

This is the first time I ever saw steps!

I tried to follow mommy up the stairs to her office but sometimes I'd get scared and get stuck.

She just picked me up, gave me kisses, and carried me with her.

Eventually, I learned how to go up *and* down by myself!

It didn't take long before I convinced my parents to let me sleep with them.

I didn't take up much room!

I would just burrow under the covers and rest my little head against their bodies.

How could they say, "no!?"

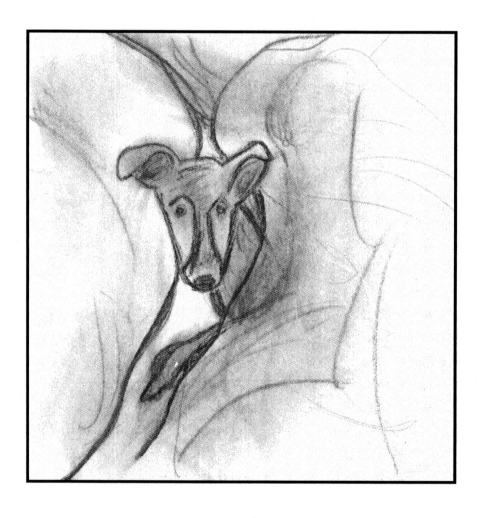

My mommy said I needed to be "social-ized" so I wasn't shy around strangers. She took me everywhere with her!

When we went to stores she either carried me under her coat or "wore me" in a puppy sack. It's like a knapsack only she wears it in front.

I got to meet lots of people. It turns out, I wasn't shy at all!

My daddy is the boss of a car dealership.

I visit him a lot and all the employees greet me saying,
  "Tony, Tony, Tony!!!"

If he's the President, does that make me the First Dog?

Christmas is a special time at our house. Mommy decorates really nice and there are lots of new things for me to explore.

I get presents!!!

People that come to see our decorations bring me gifts, too!

The only thing I didn't like was that Santa suit Mommy and Daddy thought was so cute.

I let them take a picture and then I took it off.

My parents have a grandson named Austin. He is two years old.

For Christmas Santa gave him a wooden rocking boat.

I climbed inside and played with it, too!

When I go for a walk some people whisper that I'm "skinny."

I prefer "slim and trim," myself.

Mommy loves me just the way I am and says I can't be any cuter.

She has skinny legs, too.

Mommy and Daddy are *very* considerate. Restaurants don't like me to come inside. There are rules about it.

If it is warm, they request a table outside so I can come, too.

I love to people watch!

People like to watch me, too!

They ask a lot of questions…

"What kind of dog is that?"

"Is he going to get any bigger?"

"Is it a whippet?"
(They're cousins that are a little bigger.)

"Is he very fragile?"

I should wear a sign with all the answers!

My Grandmother Helen never liked dogs…her whole life!

I think one scared her really badly when she was growing up and she's been really afraid ever since.

I changed that!

Grandmom Helen may not like ALL dogs but she LOVES me!

She lets me sleep on the couch with her and calls… *"Tony, Tony, Tony!"* when she comes to visit!

I go visiting, too!

My daddy learned to fly a plane.
They were going away for a week and couldn't take me.

My Aunt Joanne and Uncle Ronnie, who live in Atlantic City, N.J., wanted me to visit.

Daddy flew me there in his plane.

He says I'm his *"fly dog!"*

When I was visiting, we even went to New York City.

It was exciting!

I paraded around the city with my sweater that has a flag sewn on it.

I wanted all the policemen and firemen to know how proud I was of them and of being an American!

My daddy is a captain of our boat, too. It's called the *Nautiboy*.

He is *very* talented!

I have a bright yellow life preserver jacket that I wear in case I would fall into the water.

Mommy says, "You can never be too careful…"

I'm her precious son!

Mommy isn't perfect.

She made a mistake, once, by trusting that I would stay by her side while she was gardening.

I didn't.

I just ran around in the neighborhood until I found another family having a bar-beque. The food was great!

Mommy found me(having a wonderful time!) but now I can't go outside with out her and a collar and leash.

Daddy would NOT be happy if something happened to me while he was working! He says it's up to the parents to be responsible.

I wait by the window for him to come home.

As soon as I see his car come up the driveway I get SO excited. He comes in and gives me a great big greeting…

"TONY, TONY, TONY!!!"

Mommy and I both give him kisses!

Sundays are my favorite days because Daddy doesn't have to work.

Football is fun!

We watch the games on T.V. and I wear my Raven's jersey to show that we are cheering for the Baltimore Ravens.

During intermission daddy throws me the plastic football so I can practice being a star too.

When I catch it I climb up on daddy's shoulder and with my teeth make the squeaker in the toy make lots of noise.

Daddy laughs and says I'm going to give him a headache!

One of my favorite pastimes in sun-bathing. I look where the sun is shining brightest in the house and that is where I lie.

It changes during the day…and so do I!

I especially like when the sun makes a big warm patch on the rug from the window in the ceiling!

In the afternoon, the sun shines in the living room window.

That's where I take my noon nap!

Sometimes, if Grandpop is nice I let him lie with me too.

I'm a very intelligent dog but sometimes I play dumb.

Mommy will call me and I'll turn my head and pretend I don't hear a thing!

Then it gets *louder…*

"Tony, Tony, Tony!!!"

It's just a little bratty game I play!

Another one is "pull the socks."

I like to pull people's socks off their feet.

Visitors don't exactly know what to make of it. A lot of times they just let me do it.

If they don't run after me to play "catch the sock" I get bored and find something else to play with.

Daddy and granddad played a game with me, once!

They brought home a cat named Tina.

She wasn't scared of me at all which really made me mad.

The joke was that she "ran" on batteries and was a "robot!"

Ha, Ha, Ha!!!

Iggy's (like all dogs) need to go to the doctors to get regular checkups and vaccinations so they don't get sick.

I HATE NEEDLES!

You should hear me carry on...even before the doctor gives me a shot!

She said I am overdramatic.

We also need our teeth brushed…just like you!

It's not too bad because the toothpaste tastes good.

Mommy said that is "good preventative medicine."

We need to keep our teeth healthy so we can chew our food…and keep our breath smelling clean!

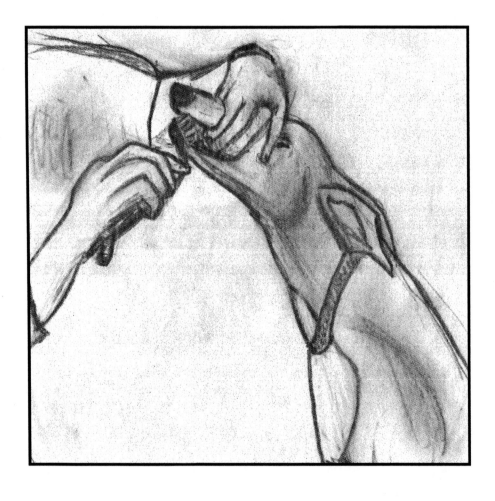

Bath time is not my favorite.

My tail goes right between my legs!

The best part is being wrapped in a warm blanket after it's all over and getting a treat!

Italian greyhounds don't have a lot of hair. That's good for people who have allergies because we don't shed or smell.

In the winter we need to wear coats or sweaters to keep warm.

You should see my wardrobe!!!

Mommy told me I don't know how lucky I am.

She explained that some families decide they don't want their pets anymore and bring them to shelters.

At night we say our prayers that they find a good home and get a second chance at happiness.

After prayers, I crawl up under the blankets to go to sleep...

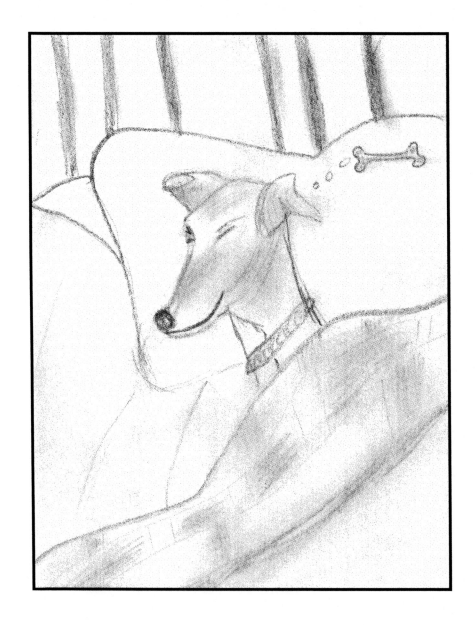

Goodnight!

Now that the children are asleep, I'd like to talk to their parents…

Italian Greyhounds are not the preferred pet for every family.

Not everyone can handle the demands of this wonderful creature who lives for love and constant companionship.

Perky and playful, this beautiful animal can be accidentally hurt by children's rough play or large pets.

Before adopting any animal, research carefully the characteristics of their breed and make sure they blend harmoniously with your lifestyle.

Animal shelters may just have the perfect pet for you and your family.

All domesticated creatures trust you implicitly and rely on you for safety and love. Their fate is in your hands.

Serve them well.

INTERESTED IN LEARNING MORE ABOUT ITALIAN GREYHOUNDS?

average height: 13-15"

Average weight: 5-15 pounds

Average life expectancy: 13 years

Dog Group: Toy Group

Coat Colors: varies

Coat Type: short, very little shedding

Disposition: very affectionate, sometimes aloof with strangers, sensitive, intelligent
Protectiveness: not very!

Trainability: can be stubborn ☺

Living space: is suitable for apartment life

Resources

American Kennel Club
260 Madison Avenue, New York, NY 20016
212 696-8200
http://www.AKC.org./

Italian Greyhound Club of America website:
http://www.italiangreyhound.org

Greyhound Pets of America
1-800-366-1472
(They will direct your call to the nearest adoption chapter)

Greyhound Protection League
415 327-0631

0-595-21879-2

Printed in the United States
54105LVS00003B/9

9 780595 218790